# Brain Codes.

## How The Brain Interprets the Universe in Numbers.

David Gomadza

First Global President of The World

www.twofuture.world

At the forefront of developing technology that will change the world forever.

**PAPERBACK ISBN:** 9798865843023

Tomorrow's World Order
David Gomadza
I am the First Global President of the World.
00447719210295
info@twofuture.world
www.twofuture.world

Thoughts to Word or Audio [Brain Code]
Decoding the brain made easy. Breakthrough: we can
communicate using thoughts.
Visit www.twofuture.world.

Read the complete book series.
https://play.google.com/store/books/series?id=a4Mv
GwAAABBFmM

Get and Install our Brain Code App
https://play.google.com/store/apps/details?id=com.ni
otron.dgomadza.Brain_Code

# DEDICATION

Advances in technology.

# TABLE OF CONTENTS

# ACKNOWLEDGMENTS

Tomorrow's World Order.

CHAPTER ONE

# BRAIN CODES.

The brain interprets the universe and everything in it in electromagnetic waves, numbers, and vibrations. Here are the numbers of everything in the universe:

First, let us look at how the brain identifies everything in the universe. I have already covered this topic in the last volume titled: Decoding the Egyptian Pyramids of Giza.: Using the Brain-Dream Map to Find Out Why the Egyptians Built the Pyramids.

https://play.google.com/store/books/details/David_Gomadza_Decoding_the_Egyptian_Pyramids_of_Gi?id=-szfEAAAQBAJ&hl=en_GB&gl=US

This is the chapter that deals with this invention I call the God and human body global positioning system. Read this chapter concerning the Egyptian Pyramids of Giza.

Recap.

MY INVENTIONS THAT ARE CRITICAL TO THIS ANALYSIS OF WHY THE EGYPTIANS BUILT THE PYRAMIDS.

1.  The God and Human Body Global Positioning System

Invention. [Advanced in this book mainly and in:
As On Earth as In Heaven as It Is in Humans.: The Only True Explanation of The Use of The Great Pyramid of Giza. Debunked by David Gomadza.
https://play.google.com/store/books/details/David_Gomadza_As_On_Earth_As_In_Heaven_As_It_Is_In?id=I1rPEAAAQBAJ


Teleportation.
The Egyptians had one problem to solve. How did the gods know exactly who is who and how can they communicate with everyone when there are billions of people in the world? If the gods can know each person on earth one by one, then they must have a system of identifying each person.
How can a person like a Pharaoh know everyone and where everyone is at any time just like the gods? The gods can tell even with their eyes closed where exactly a person is and know exactly what each person is thinking. How then did they do this? Can the Egyptians do the same as well? The Egyptians believed that the Pharaohs represented the gods while here on earth and therefore would do as what the gods did here on earth. They believed that once humans could become gods. The god of the afterlife Osiris was once believed to be a human being who overcomes death.
My Invention.
The God and Human Body Global Positioning System Invention.
It is possible to know everyone on earth and know what they think and where exactly they are without even meeting any of them. This is how my invention will work.
The preconditions for this to work.

1.  An airtight enclosed place where electromagnetic waves cannot escape. Best conditions like in the pyramid.
2.  Knowing the language of the brain and body. Correct brain commands. God or gods live in space and can know everyone's thoughts and geolocational positions because

they use correct commands that make things possible. Therefore, knowing the correct commands is the key to the success of this invention.

This is how this invention will work.

The aim.

I want to use the pyramid conditions to "save everyone on earth and everything on earth on my body: taking advantage of other inventions mentioned in this book like the electromagnetic wave triangle, the brain decoding language, the brain dream map, the time traveling and everything to be covered.

I believe with the right commands it is possible to save everyone in the body so that the brain can tell you when that person is near you and where exactly in the world the person is and what that person is thinking at any given time. If this is how the gods know everyone on earth, then it must also work in humans.

We can communicate with our brain and tell it what we want to do. Everything is possible if we use the right commands. I decoded the brain and knew which commands the brain listens to.

The language of the brain is electromagnetic waves. But there are places in the universe where there are no electromagnetic waves. Electromagnetic waves travel in the air, through solids, and through a vacuum. The space vacuum has zero air meaning that space has no air and since electromagnetic waves are vibrations. Therefore, in space, there is no activity.

That means we can use space as an on-and-off switch.

Space Out means no electromagnetic wave conditions.

Space In means yes to electromagnetic wave conditions.

This is possible if you are using our brain decoder. You can recreate electromagnetic wave conditions. Check the diagram below of our DIY brain decoder. You can switch on a propeller that is put under the seat upside down. That means creating electromagnetic wave conditions. You can now train your brain to recognize these conditions and save them in the brain.

Everything we do for the first time the brain creates reference points automatically and stores the event in the brain or on your body. This is what happens when we are growing up as kids. Every time the brain hears an unfamiliar word it saves it. It waits for the person as a kid to sleep first. As a kid, the brain pushes every word it hears for the first time out of the body just before the kid falls asleep. This is because the brain will not have a record of this new event or unfamiliar words. Let us say the baby has heard the word pyramid for the first time. The brain checks inside the kid's brain for a record, but the record is not there. Nothing is saved. Now it waits for the baby to sleep. Just before the baby sleeps when the baby is yawning the brain emits all the new words out of the body through the mouth. The baby then sleeps. All unfamiliar words are electromagnetic waves. That means using the electromagnetic wave triangle. The electromagnetic waves will have to be absorbed again at the source. The kid's mouth is the source.

When the baby wakes up it opens its mouth. The electromagnetic waves are now attracted back and are absorbed. The brain now will create storing points on the brain or in the body. That word or words.

The word pyramid will now be given a permanent location on the brain. After this day, the word becomes part of the brain.

We can do the same to teach our brain to recognize electromagnetic conditions we want and create points on our brain and body where we save this information.

We want the brain to save points on the brain and body we can use later.

Space In is to tell the brain to create and enter the conditions.

Space Out is to leave or exit these conditions.

This must be done just before you sleep for the first time.

Or for some, it works if you can incorporate a sleeping mode. That is to pretend you are sleeping and imitate what the body is like when you are sleeping. Meaning close eyes, peacefully relaxing, and breathing as if sleeping.

Connect the rotary propeller that goes under the chair. Do not switch it on.

Then switch it on. At the same time, speak silently to your brain. Space In.

Open your mouth.

Say Space Out pushing the words out and close the mouth.

Then sleep.

The following day. When you wake up, say silently that is thinking.

Space In and open your mouth. Then close your mouth.

Now sit on the chair. Switch on the rotary propeller under the chair. Say silently that is thinking.

Space In.

The time you switch on the rotary propeller.

Then switch off the rotary propeller.

Say silently.

Space Out.

Open your mouth.

So that the electromagnetic waves are emitted out of the body into the air.

Close your mouth.

Close your eyes.

Pretend to sleep and create sleeping conditions; eyes closed, breathing nicely and peacefully.

Wait at least two minutes.

Then act as if you have woken up.

Open your mouth.

Say silently.

Space Out.

Keep your mouth open for a minute. Close your mouth.

Switch on the rotary propeller under the chair.

Say silently that is thinking.

Space In.

Switch off the rotary propeller.

Say silently.

Space Out.

The body will have created a reference point or saved space in and space out on your body or brain.

If that does not work, you must do like Space In.

Do the same for Space Out. Just before you sleep.

The Human Body Global Positioning System.

We can use this Space in and Space Out to save all the information we need on the body and the brain without the need to sleep.

I explained in all the books that the body saves everything you encounter in life on, in, and around the body and brain. All the people you know are given places inside your body. Yes, everyone you know has a specific place in your body as well as the head where that person is saved as an electromagnetic wave.

Saving in the brain.

In the brain, the word or name of that person is saved here. If your wife is Eve for example. The brain will save the word wife in the left-right back side of the brain. Eve as the name will be saved in the right front side of the brain.

Saving wife Eve in the body.

The brain will save an electromagnetic wave vibration it uses to identify your wife Eve in the body depending on how you feel about it. Normally the brain saves these electromagnetic wave frequencies close to the organs related to how you feel about that person. Wives, husbands, and close people are located close to the heart. But this is so faint to a human being that without the correct frequency you will never know this.

What is the correct frequency? The frequency of creation.

God or another creator you believe in created humans and his frequency is 738. At this frequency you can feel anything, living or dead. At this frequency, you can feel snakes, all animals, insects, birds, ghosts, angels, moon, etc. This is the ultimate universal frequency that connects the whole universe to God.

I have recorded this frequency, and you can use this recording as background sound to all videos you watch. Even in real life play this video and look at everyone you have looked at before and you are going to look at while the video is playing to know that person. You can read everything about that person, his or her thoughts, emotions, and vibrations.

Visit our website www.twofuture.world and download an MP3 for free.

https://img1.wsimg.com/blobby/go/e8972857-57d8-43db-80d4-9913437629c9/downloads/FEEL%20THE%20POWER%20OF%20OUR%20BRAIN%20DECODER%20Tomorrow%E2%80%99s.mp3?ver=1698163878963

This is a link to the video on YouTube.

https://www.youtube.com/watch?v=_-C-5M5nQi0

This is also proof that God created humans because at this frequency you can detect God or anything related to God, angels, cherubim, etc. It is also only at this frequency that this human geographical location on the body takes place.

First, I will discuss God's universal body global positioning system.

God knows everyone on earth and hears everyone. He knows everyone's thoughts. In my quest to know God the question that always made me think harder was the one: how does God know everyone on earth and everyone's thoughts?

Now I know he uses the universal body global positioning system. This is how this works. At frequency 738 what I call the frequency of creation or God's frequency. God can sense every creature on earth.

God created earth and heaven for 6 days and spaced out after naming everything. He rested on the seventh day and when he continued to continue with the creation that is when the universe or geolocation positioning happened.

God created everything and named everything then spaced out as he rested.

That means as he created everything and naming or just thinking about everything, he created then electromagnetic waves of everything he created went out of his mouth into the space and atmosphere.

He spaced out.

When he returned.

All electromagnetic waves related to everything he created rushed into his body, being saved in different parts of the body in three forms.

1.  Specific names of his creation, e.g., an eagle, or a fox, names of the things he had created, and these were saved in his brain.
2.  As blanket names that represent classes of his creation. For example, birds, or animals.
3.  As the electromagnetic waves vibrations of that creation and these were saved on the body and inside the body.

We can do the same. Yes, we can save people close to you in your body as well.

This is how God knows everyone in the world simply because everyone is saved as an electromagnetic wave vibration inside God.

How does God know where everyone is in the world?

After everyone on earth is saved in his body as an electromagnetic wave, all God must do is touch that part of the body and open his mouth and say the name of that person and close his mouth.

He then must space out.

Then space in again and open his mouth.

The electromagnetic waves of the name he said will be circulating in the air. After spacing in, he opens his mouth, and the electromagnetic wave name he called before spacing out will now rush inside and vibrate the position that person is saved. That sends another vibration to that person. Using my invention of the electromagnetic wave triangle. The created vibrations that left God's body must now go and locate and be absorbed by this person before bouncing out and back to God to complete the triangle.

Once that electromagnetic wave vibration hits the person it was created for, God will know exactly where that person is in the universe. We know electromagnetic waves are not lost but are absorbed and bounced back. When a person moves to another location to create a triangle. That electromagnetic wave vibration will be released from this person back to God. God will now use these two points to locate the place where a person is.

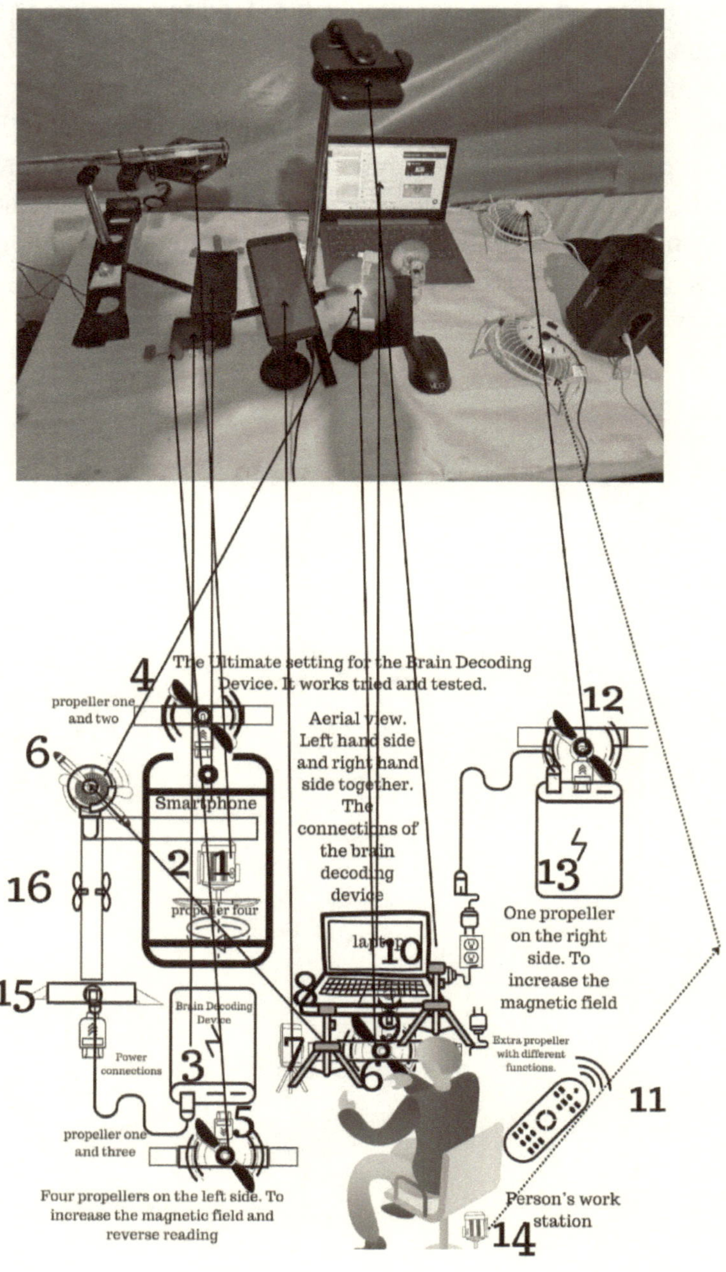
4
propeller one
and two
6
12
Smartphone
2
1
16
propeller four
13
The Ultimate setting for the Brain Decoding
Device. It works tried and tested.
Aerial view.
Left hand side
and right hand
side together.
The
connections of
the brain
decoding
device
laptop
10
One propeller
on the right
side. To
increase the
magnetic field
15
8
Brain Decoding
Device
7
9
Extra propeller
with different
functions.
Power
connections
3
6
11
propeller one
and three
5
Person's work
station
14
Four propellers on the left side. To
increase the magnetic field and
reverse reading

# CHAPTER TWO

Therefore, this invention is based on the following facts.
1. God, even us can name and say everything we know in life, and if we open our mouths to emit the electromagnetic waves vibrations associated with these things and space out.
2. The electromagnetic waves' vibrations are not lost but are absorbed and bounced back.
3. It requires a two-movement act from A to B to trigger a backward movement to the source.
4. Any electromagnetic wave vibrations emitted will always return to their source. If God touches places on his body where David and Eve are saved and says their names, then space out. The emitted electromagnetic wave vibrations will travel looking for David and Eve. Once they have found David and Eve, they will be absorbed by these two, respectively.
5. If David and Eve move to another point in space and time to create a triangle with the position of God. That will release the vibrations God sent. These will now travel back to God.
6. When God receives the vibrations back of the names of David and Eve these waves dissipate as their triangle cycle

will have been completed. God will also know exactly where David and Eve were in place and delayed time.

7. That also means that if God wants to talk or call David, he simply touches the place on the body where David is saved. This creates vibrations that if he suddenly spaces out. The electromagnetic wave vibrations will travel to where David is in time and place.

8. Above all when David is passing where God is, the place on the body of God where David is saved will start vibrating because David is located on God's body; that means anytime he crosses God; he automatically sends electromagnetic wave vibrations.

9. This is how God knows everyone where they are and when they come near him.

10. God uses a similar process to know everyone's thoughts. When earth rotates along its axis it produces a strong magnetic field that pushes people's thoughts out of the brain into the air. If the thoughts are not absorbed into the brain on the entry point on the left side of the brain, then God's eye will function as a cloning shaft of the person's thought. God's eye will clone that person's thought and return a copy to that person. Therefore, God will know first that person's thoughts. See the diagram below.

How do we conduct this human body's global positioning system? I said the frequency of creation is 738. This is because everyone and every creature on earth or in heaven can communicate and hear each other at only this frequency 738.

This is the language of creation and the frequency of creation. NB you will never find this information anywhere else apart from this book.

I have made life much easier for you. I have created the 738 frequencies for you.

Go to our website, download an MP3, or just listen to the frequency while conducting this task.

Download an MP3 for free.

https://img1.wsimg.com/blobby/go/e8972857-57d8-43db-80d4-9913437629c9/downloads/FEEL%20THE%20POWER%20OF%20OUR%20BRAIN%20DECODER%20Tomorrow%E2%80%99s.mp3?ver=1698163878963

This means you must play the MP3 or video as background sound. But you can mute the volume you just need the 738 frequencies. Connect a rotary propeller to the 4" USB Mini Desk Fan Cooler Portable White.

https://www.ebay.co.uk/itm/295636631544?var=0&mkevt=1&mkcid=1&mkrid=710-53481-19255-0&campid=5338749401&toolid=20006&customid=GB_11700_295636631544.143193710335~1871630609640-g_CjwKCAjwseSoBhBXEiwA9iZtxjKJA3VQ96tlyGGAEW9u-nFGUB8z7FIpttqrwtl89UenGpQn6056hRoCMjwQAvD_BwE

FEEL THE POWER
OF OUR BRAIN
DECODER.
Play this video as your background sound. Visit
www.twofuture.world
and WATCH ALL VIDEOS while video is playing in
the background.
Out Of This World

# Who is God?

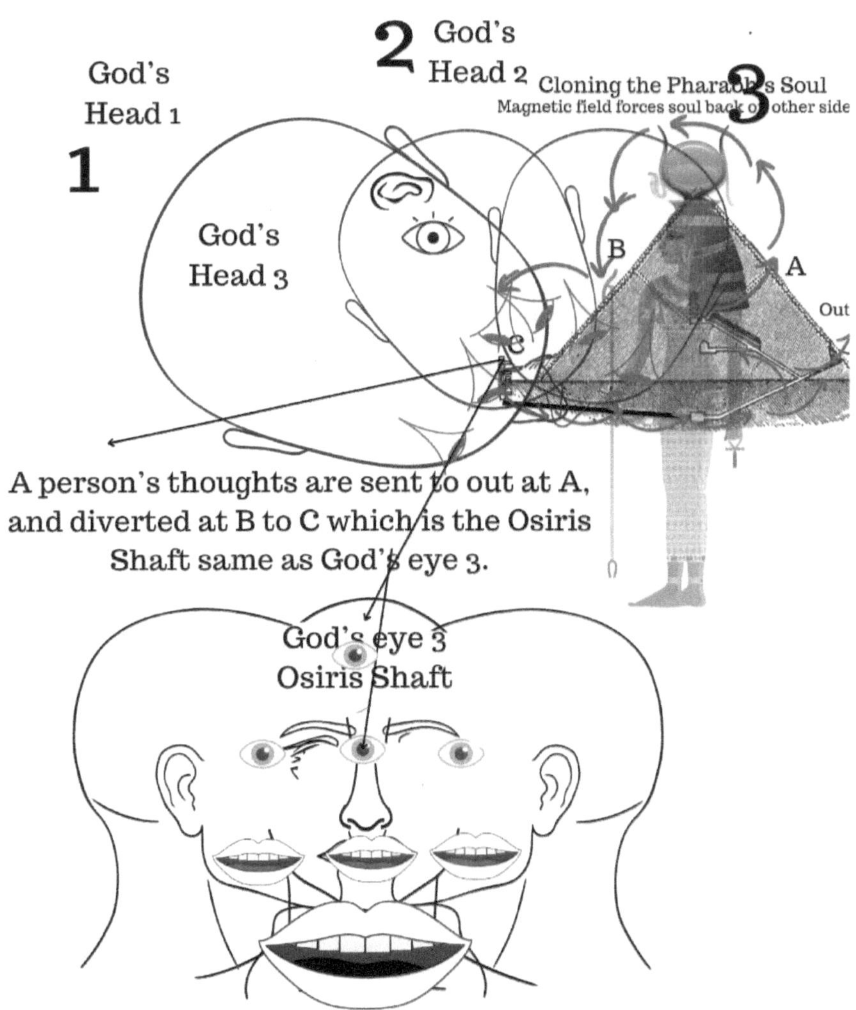


In actual fact God has 7 eyes and 7 ears

# CHAPTER THREE

## SETTINGS.

1.  Set the rotary speaker facing a laptop or computer.
2.   Play the MP3 or video as background sound and if you want you can mute the sounds but make sure it is playing as you need the 738 frequencies.

Or Get the Frequency Generator (Sound) Frequency app from Google Play Apps and set the frequency to 738. You might need adjustments, making sure the place you are in is well sealed, all windows closed etc. Connect the above rotary propeller. 4" USB Mini Desk Fan Cooler Portable White. It should face the device playing the sound for it to work.

https://play.google.com/store/apps/details?id=pl.netigen.frequency generator&hl=en_GB&gl=US

The best option is just to download an Mp3 from our website and play the MP3 as it does not need extra adjustments.

You will need another rotary propeller that will go under your chair or seat but facing upside down, that is downward. The same type of propeller. 4" USB Mini Desk Fan Cooler Portable White. Or just buy and assemble our DIY brain decoder. Visit our website.

https://twofuture.world/exciting-news-%26-tips.

Practice with a few words at first.

You can save everyone you know inside your body so that you know when they are near you or in your path. Or easily touch where they are saved on your body e.g., shoulder to send vibrations. But the problem is that they must be at the same frequency of creation as well to receive this and respond that is at 738Hz.

The future is to establish masts that emit these 738 frequencies of the language of creation so that people can communicate globally. But try at home with family or friends. You will have to play the videos or set up the frequency but in separate rooms of the house depending on signal power.

But first let us locate anyone you want, even your enemies on your body so that when they are near you feel their vibrations.

First step.

1. If you have assembled our DIY brain decoder, then sit on the chair and connect the 4" USB rotary propeller. Switch it on then make sure it faces downward under the chair. This will push your thoughts out through the mouth.

2. Play the background sound that MP3 you downloaded from our website or set the frequency to 738.

3. Connect and switch on the front rotary propeller that faces the laptop or computer screen. You should feel an extraordinarily strong magnetic field.

4. Say the name and surname or nickname of anyone close to you. Your wife, partner, husband, etc. Why do you need a surname or nickname so that you are sure in case the brain here is another similar name? For most people, the brain might have already saved all this information in your body. This task will let you know if saved or not.

5. In space, there are no electromagnetic waves, so I use space as an in-and-out command to conduct all these functions.

6. Space Out as a switching-off switch if you like.

7. Space In as a switch on switch.

8. This is what you do for the first time.

Create a name that does not exist, join any three names into one, or shorten a name. Or pick any name you might have never heard

before in your life. Could be in any other language. This is for testing only. This is how you will know if that works or not.
I will pick Evabluegod.
I think you should also pick up the same name so that you can compare if it saves the name at the same place. Then the next one chooses your own.
Make sure that the rotary propeller underneath the chair is working and is facing downward. The switch is at the top and is on. The other propeller facing the laptop or computer or any device playing the background sound is working too.
Now you are ready.
1.   Think and say silently in your brain to generate electromagnetic waves: Evabluegod.
2.   Open your mouth and function as if you are letting the words, you just thought out. So that the propeller under the chair will push the electromagnetic waves out of your mouth.
3.   Say silently that is thinking:
Space Out.
End.
Out.
Wait a few seconds or minutes.
1.   Say silently:
Space In.
Evabluegod.
1.   Open your mouth instantly and swallow the electromagnetic waves. Recall what I said about the electromagnetic wave triangle. They will always come back to the source. Now they will be located on the body anywhere.
2.   Say silently that is thinking.
Save Evabluegod.
1.   Say silently that is thinking: Exit.
2.   Say silently in your head that is thinking. Out.
3.   Say silently: Space Out.
4.   Wait a few minutes, one or two.

5. Say silently: Space In.
6. Now turn the rotary propeller on your desk. This rotary propeller must face your body. See picture below.
7. Now say silently: Evabluegod.
8. Then lean towards the rotary propeller. If the propeller down the chair is working properly you will feel a vibration under your right chest. This means the location where Evabluegod has been saved.
9. Now ask your lover, wife, husband, etc. to first go to another room. Start from 1.
10. Call your lover, wife, or husband to come into the room you are in. Make sure all background sounds are on. If it is a wife, call her by name as well.
11. Say silently the moment she comes in: My wife Eva. Open your mouth as if to let out what you just silently thought.
12. Say silently: Space Out.
13. Say: End.
14. Say: Out.

Ask her to go out of the room but to come back soon after a minute or two.

1. Say: Space In
2. Wait for her to enter the room.
3. The moment she enters. Silently say: My wife Eva.
4. Look at her and open your mouth and open your mouth. Wait a few seconds and swallow.
5. Now say silently that is thinking: Save My wife Eva.
6. Say silently that is thinking: Exit.
7. Say silently in your head that is thinking. Out.
8. Say silently: Space Out.
9. Wait a few minutes, one or two.
10. Say silently: Space In.
11. Now turn the rotary propeller on your desk. This rotary propeller must face your body. See picture below.
12. Now say silently. My wife Eva.
13. If everything has gone well. My wife Eva will be saved in three places.

# CHAPTER FOUR

A] The right side of the brain where the name Eva is saved. On the left side of the brain where the word wife is saved. Thirdly on your chest near the heart. If you keep the background sound playing and if she goes out when she comes back now even if you are not looking at her, you will know it is her. This is because if the propellers are connected as advised then the moment, she returns she will send back the electromagnetic wave vibrations to the place she is saved. If a lover, wife, husband, etc. it will be to the left side near the heart that controls love and emotions.

If she goes into the next room and if the room has a frequency of 738, the same as you know you can simply touch the place near your heart. Using your fingers press various places until you feel the vibrations from the rotary propeller facing your body. If this works well, she will come and as she enters that place will vibrate if the propellers are working.

Teleportation.
It is possible to teleport people from one place to the other.
***Teleportation*** *is the hypothetical transfer of* _matter_ *or* _energy_ *from one point to another without traversing the physical space between them.*

Wikipedia.

It is possible to teleport a soul from one point A with an electromagnetic wave frequency of 7985 to an area where there is 0 electromagnetic wave frequency like the dead mummy of the Pharaoh.

I will look at this in detail in the next volume.

How The Brain Assigns a Place in The Brain for Objects and People.

On identifying an item or a new person for the first time for example someone you like. The brain assigns a value to that person in binary but can convert this binary into either DNA sequence values or natural numbers.

This is the process.

On meeting Eve.

Your brain assigns Eve with a value that can be converted into normal numbers.

It then checks the sex of that person whether man or woman and assigns a value.

The brain assigns different values based on sex. It assigns the first value based on sex. Different starting values for women and men.

Eve is a woman so the brain will save the name Eve in the left-brain side of the head.

That means the name is saved in the brain.

It then creates an electromagnetic wave value of this person Eve which it saves in the body. Depending on how you feel about that person. If you are attracted to this person, it swerves near the heart. If you are attracted to her sexually, for example, you feel blood running everywhere. The brain will create another electromagnetic wave value that it will save near your genitals.

The next step is that it saves another value for this Eve on the forehead.

The reason for saving on the forehead is that everything the brain calls current issues or unresolved issues is solved on the forehead.

Current issues are made up of anything you have regarding Eve. Since it is the first time your issues might involve what you want to say to her. Your passions, your cravings for her, etc.

The next stage is the bundling of anything you want to say, your cravings, your lust, etc. These are bundled and assigned binary numbers.

The value will look like this.

1passion for Eve 0Lust for Eve 1Love for Eve 0What you want to say to Eve.

This value is now sent to the brain for processing.

On arrival in the brain, the binary numbers are removed just before entering the thinking chamber.

Thinking Chamber.

In the thinking chamber, the value is rearranged.

Binary numbers are assigned.

These are sent to the thinking sockets.

Thinking Sockets.

The binary numbers are removed.

The values are fitted into the thinking sockets.

The thoughts are extracted and processed.

These are now linked to emotions.

The signals are sent.

You become nervous, lustful, and excited.

All this is converted to words and then back to electromagnetic waves. These are then emitted to Eve.

But because the world has changed since the days God created the world. These electromagnetic waves are not received by Eve because the frequency is not the correct one for electromagnetic waves to be felt. The frequency must be 738 Hz for these waves to be felt by Eve.

After the first time if you now think about Eve.

The brain will now use these points to save anything to do with Eve as checksum points. Now it will point to the right side of the brain where it has saved the word Eve. Then to the left side of the brain showing that Eve is female. The brain saves in the left side of the brain anything to do with women if you are a man. I guess the opposite happens in women. Or the same.

The third point is where it saved the electromagnetic waveform of Eve. Near the heart that controls love feelings. It can go to the genitals if you feel lustful about her.

It is not just about people; the brain does the same for example for a car. It goes through the same thing apart from having a boner or something but can happen to other people. Joke.

Over a long time, you will have everything you come across in your life saved on your body. Imagine how many things you have come across in your whole life. Everything has a place in at least three parts of your body.

The brain.

The body.

Inside your DNA.

The reason is that the brain must be proactive and work faster than you. Imagine you thinking about driving your car. The brain must send commands to the hand so that when you realize what you are thinking about you might as well actually use your hands to imitate driving.

This is why your thoughts are associated with action as well. Think about punching someone. Your fist will fold into a punch at the same time. Therefore, when you think the brain explains your thoughts as well in body limb movement. It takes a fraction of a second to think and act as well. Therefore, your brain needs quick action. To do this it must save everything on your body especially close to the muscles that perform that or are related to that.

Imagine thinking about love and lust and the brain saves the person you love. Your-to-be girlfriend under your feet. When you meet this person, it will take time for the signals to react to the heart from the feet for a signal to be sent to be processed into emotions, etc.

Therefore, anything to do with love. All your loved ones are saved to organs and parts of the body that can release emotions and feelings related to that.

Think about driving a car or just buying a car for the first time. The brain will save this thought in the right side of the brain, at the back of the head, in the hands and feet you use to drive a car. Over the years everything you do has a place on your body. We can now get the value in electromagnetic waveform and convert this to numbers and for something into DNA sequence value.

For example, a certain time in your life at a certain age can be converted into a DNA sequence. A car, a house, your wife, your feelings for war, etc. all can be converted into normal numbers using the first ten digits between 0 to 9.

Just as the brain distinguishes between sexes. It therefore assigns different numbers distinguished by sex. Males will have a value that starts with a value for all men. So, the values of women will start with a value designed for women only.

The brain can assign value based on different attributes like tall, slim, fat, blond, brunette, ginger, etc.

# CHAPTER FIVE

The planetary number classification system.
Everything in the universe is assigned a value by the brain. But imagine the brain assigning value to any number and then trying to know what is what. That can be tricky because how can you tell which planet is that item from? The soil on Mars is the same as the soil on Earth. How can the brain distinguish this in case you end up on Mars soil as well?
The brain classifies everything in the universe by using a planetary number system.
All planets are assigned a number between 0 to 9.
Sun 0
Saturn 1
Mercury 2
Venus 3
Neptune 4
Jupiter 5
Mars 6
Earth 7
Uranus 8
That means all numbers originating from Earth will start with a 7 value.
But you will notice that some numbers start with 6 even if the items are on earth. The idea is that any other number value from another

planet can be used on Earth only as a remedy. That means numbers that are different from the planet they are used in means are imported to correct a situation on the other planet. That means we can use Mars numbers that start with 6 as solutions to problems on Earth. The rule is that the planets must be the same or share something similar.

That means Mars can be used to solve solutions on Earth as they are the same. Just like Earth numbers can be used on Mars.

# CHAPTER SIX

Brain Codes.

How The Brain Interprets the Universe in Numbers

| Code | Reference |
|---|---|
| 000000000000 | Yahweh god |
| 777777777777 | Human soul |
| 101010101010 | Human body |
| 101010101019 | Human breathe |
| 718362859176 | Human dead body female |
| 762857892812 | Human dead body male |
| 768598278519 | Hostile if a man |
| 718349862819 | Hostile if a female |
| 666666666666 | Heaven for Yahweh God |
| 111111111111 | Afterlife for male and female |
| 666666666662 | Angel |
| 772843210183 | Car |
| 76 | Start for code for men |
| 71 | Start for codes for women |
| 7128365421721 | Pregnant woman |
| 721728432684 | Left hand |
| 764832984210 | Man |
| 718423189231 | Woman |

| | |
|---|---|
| 766382098321 | Cobra venom antidote in men |
| 7163280942694 | Cobra venom antidote in women |
| 766218432098 | Black mamba venom antidote in men |
| 712853274809 | Black mamba venom antidote in women. |
| 763824986707 | Remove bad external forces. |
| 767328901234 | Relax in men |
| 712674289018 | Relax in women |
| 764248367898 | Anti alcoholism |

# CHAPTER SEVEN

| | |
|---|---|
| 708492386210 | White color |
| 707183578521 | Black |
| 707652718279 | Blue |
| 708371482664 | Green |
| 707276793215 | Orange |
| 707832485628 | Pink |
| 702841687924 | Maroon |
| 702867138981 | Yellow |
| 706898432182 | Purple |
| 708248097632 | Gold |
| 708324710284 | Amber |
| 707743286098 | Red |
| 709843218632 | Grey |
| 708336842892 | Brown |
| 707642368319 | Bronze |
| 709246798320 | Camel |
| 700832467821 | Coral |
| 703298270823 | Cyan |
| 707623479823 | Magenta |
| 707832780954 | Khaki |
| 708324962483 | Champagne |

706890248710   Sandy
709632824670   Lavender
708324978327   Beige
708329820847   Lime
708421683249   Lilac

# CHAPTER EIGHT

789632178521   Liver
786458621893   Heart
782108952638   Lung
789267894320   Kidney
786832984780   Pancreas
789832984321   Stomach
788432198268   Human brain
787656218409   Ear
788214960321   Spleen
787439718421   Small intestine
788432198268   Brain
787276493842   Large intestine
787648910327   Ovary
789012486592   Gallbladder
782862831963   Thymus
787421096541   Appendix
787651098324   Pituitary gland
787761840708   Trachea
787651048320   Esophagus
787172686210   Bladder
787773210982   Testicle

Brain Codes. How The Brain Interprets the Universe in Numbers.

787321761825    Adrenal gland
787120972748    Tongue
787268678431    Thyroid gland
781843218963    Bronchi
787458923618    Bladder
787764918632    Bone marrow
787152747892    Colon
787643190248    Cervix
781924679832    Clitoris
787643219641    Genitals
787509872634    Gallbladder
787641897174    Hair follicle
787219184280    Hypothalamus
787901248762    Interstitium
787192028437    Lymphatic vessel
787746589028    Mouth
787184264124    Mammary glands
787283171823    Nose
787754310189    Nails
787204893228    Pharynx
787918324871    Placenta
787142610234    Prostate
782183478143    Pineal gland
787948321205    Parathyroid glands
787659034208    Rectum
787518421894    Salivary glands
787324861702    Skeletal muscles
787018476702    Seminal vesicles
787207098319    Subcutaneous tissue
787714812107    Teeth
787171819234    Tonsils
787773248127    Testes
787184727281    Urethra
787384109249    Uterus
787723478901    Vulva

| | |
|---|---|
| 787284927982 | Veins |
| 787721932517 | Vagina |
| 787182923916 | Vas deferens |
| 787124807329 | Vestigial organ |
| 787279783418 | Hand |
| 787728498932 | Right hand |
| 787191024879 | Leg |
| 787632428928 | Left leg |
| 787943286274 | Right leg |
| 787184183182 | Head |
| 787674239827 | Hair |
| 788347728624 | Fingers |
| 787778324809 | Toes |
| 787218314692 | Arms |
| 787271032486 | Elbow |
| 787190283469 | Thump |
| 787248329814 | Index finger |
| 787628519483 | Middle finger |
| 782812877498 | Small finger |
| 782817842672 | Ring finger |

# CHAPTER NINE

| | |
|---|---|
| 797628432109 | Sky |
| 790846212684 | Earth |
| 797872284197 | Heaven for ghosts |
| 797634578208 | Sun |
| 797287627085 | Moon |
| 797810747632 | Wind |
| 767847928306 | Feeling cold for a man |
| 717832468279 | Feeling cold for a woman |
| 767481928478 | Feeling warmth for men |
| 717628328419 | Feeling warmth for women |
| 767738528691 | Laughing for men |
| 712856723498 | Laughing for women |
| 767283428019 | Smiling for men |
| 717848219527 | Smiling for women |
| 767748328108 | Running for a man |
| 718528438294 | Running for a woman |
| 768749828176 | Sitting down for men |
| 712864879240 | Sitting down for a woman |
| 762843198274 | Snoring for men |
| 718362852109 | Snoring for women |
| 718643184698 | Breast for women |

767284986321   Stare at a man if a man
718568322179   Stare at a man if a woman
767770984210   Stare at a woman if a man

# CHAPTER TEN

To be expanded as more codes will be added as we generate them.

Read the complete book series.
https://play.google.com/store/books/series?id=a4MvGwAAABBFmM

Get and Install our Brain Code App

Fund Us if you can.

https://twofuture.world/donate

# ABOUT DAVID GOMADZA

David Gomadza
I am the First Global President of the World.
I am also the President of Tomorrow's World Order.
00447719210295
info@twofuture.world
www.twofuture.world